FEELINGS
INSIDE YOU & OUTLOUD TOO

FEELINGS
INSIDE YOU & OUTLOUD TOO

Author: Barbara Kay Polland, Ph.D.
Photographer: Craig De Roy

CELESTIALARTS

Berkeley, California

First Printing, January 1975
Made in the United States of America

Library of Congress Cataloging in Publication data

Polland, Barbara Kay, 1939-
    Feelings: inside you and out loud, too.

    SUMMARY: Explores various feelings and emotions and
discusses how to express and deal with them.
      1. Emotions—Juvenile literature. 2. Communication
—Psychological aspects—Juvenile literature.
[1. Emotions] I. DeRoy, Craig, ill. II. Title.
BF723.E6P64   152.4   74-25835
ISBN 0-89087-006-3

      9 10 11 - 93 92 91

FOREWORD

In describing people we meet, we usually do so in categories: physical, mental, emotional and so on. He or she is nice-looking, overweight, tall; bright, slow-witted, well-informed; quick-tempered, good-natured, amiable. But these quick reactions are only our perceptions of a small part of what might or might not constitute the person. Human beings are so complex that we are always dividing them into bits and pieces of the whole in simplistic attempts to understand them.

Even though we know such divisions are arbitrary, that the pieces cannot be understood apart from the whole and that the whole can be only dimly and incompletely known from the pieces, we nonetheless perceive and think about people in such terms. Sometimes, we carry this segmented thinking to such extremes that gross distortions occur. Such is the case with much of what goes on under the name of education.

It requires only a little reflection to conclude that all of these components are essential to the well-being of the whole; that physical, mental and emotional health go hand in hand. All must be preserved and, to the degree possible, enhanced. And yet, when we think of education and schooling, we think first and foremost about the mental component—and, often, as though this bears little relationship to anything else. The materials, techniques and especially the tests are geared to what educators call "cognition."

Only recently have we come to realize that a hungry, ill-nourished child cannot pay optimal attention to what is designed to stimulate cognition. We are even more backward with regard to his feelings. Presumably, they are to be kept well in check, especially in school. Educational programs designed to help children develop greater awareness of their feelings and, indeed, to develop increased sensitivities and alternate modes of expressing them are a rarity.

Since it will be some years before such programs become standard fare in most schools, we must look elsewhere for opportunities to provide children with appropriate stimuli. In what follows, Barbara Polland gives us one such opportunity. And since feelings arise from and must be worked out in association with others, this book should be appealing to parents seeking a bridge between their own and their children's feelings. It is a vehicle designed to carry both parent and child on a voyage together.

Barbara Polland points a necessary direction for education. It involves, first, the recognition and acceptance that feelings exist and that getting them out is a first step in dealing with them constructively. For a long time, children were not to be heard. Then, their feelings were not to be heard. Now, we are developing some awareness of the need to take a next step: feelings can be educated.

—Dr. John I. Goodland, Professor & Dean
  Graduate School of Education, UCLA
  and
  Director of Research, Institute for Development
  of Educational Activities, Inc.

Thank you to National College of Education, Evanston, Illinois, an institution filled with beautiful people who so facilitated my dream of becoming a teacher. And to the sensitive caring of Helen Kove, Reverend Richard Johnson, Edith Sullwold, and my family who have given me opportunities to experience feelings inside me and outloud too!

B.K.P.

How often have each of us remarked, "If I had only said that at the time!"? Keeping in touch with our feelings and projecting effective responses takes real effort. The purpose of this book is to begin long before adulthood to understand our emotions, the cause and effect of interactions.

We expect children to scream, withdraw, fight, pout, and hit, and these outbursts do have their place in childhood. How do we, as adults, usually react to these outbursts? We quickly learn how to change the subject, offer some kind of bribe, or anything else that will swiftly move the child away from the undesirable behavior. Are we underestimating children? More often we need to try staying with the feelings that are pouring out and help children find constructive channels or alternative solutions.

Children and adults experience themselves more positively if they can get in touch with what they are feeling, why, and then have the tools to respond effectively. *Feelings — Inside You and Outloud Too*, is offered as one avenue for adults and children to exchange inner feelings and reflections in a sharing, caring growing atmosphere.

—Barbara Kay Polland

For my treasures: Peter, Mark and Tamy!

FEELINGS
INSIDE YOU & OUTLOUD TOO

It doesn't matter if you are *VERY BIG* or very little, you have *Feelings — Inside You and Outloud Too!* And no one in the whole world can know what you are feeling inside unless you decide to let them.

There are many ways to feel and this book will help you to think and talk about ten of them:

1. Special
2. Frustrated
3. Private
4. Fear
5. Love
6. Pain
7. Good
8. Jealous
9. Close
10. Alone

It is so important to understand *why* you feel the way you do but there is something else important too . . . . . If you want to *tell* someone how you are feeling there are many different ways to do it. Explore some of the ways as you go through this book.

Special

It's great to be with people who make you feel super to be you!

What do they do to make you feel *sooooo* special?

Frustrated

Sometimes learning new things is hard.

Do you ever yell at someone, "Leave me alone, I can do it myself!"?

Try explaining that inside feeling
of just knowing that pretty soon you'll get it.

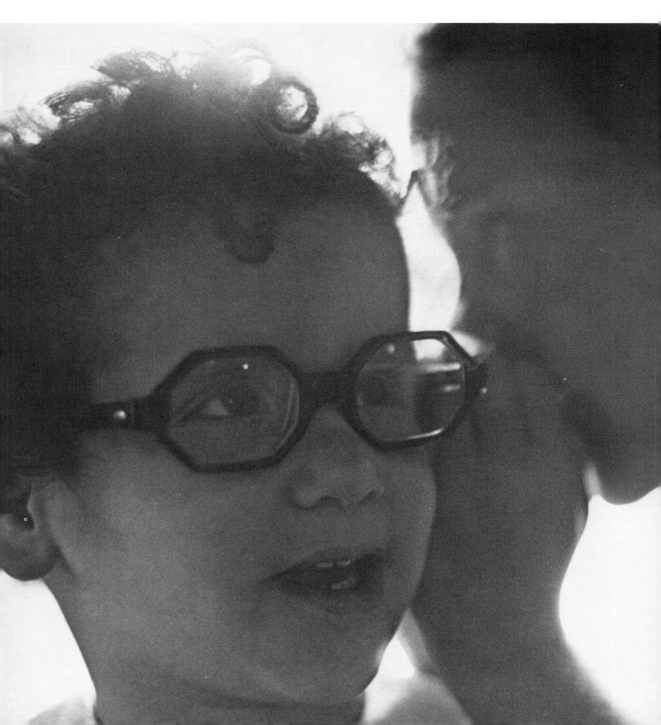

Private

Why does it feel so good to know a secret?

Who do you trust with your shhhh private thoughts?

Fear

Can you think of three things you used to be afraid of but aren't anymore?

Why do you stop being afraid of some things?

Love

Make a list of all the kinds of things you love, like people, music, toys, and holidays.

Do you love these things in different ways?

Make up any story you want
about this picture and
when you are finished
just say, "the end."

Find someone else
to tell you *their own* story
about this picture.

Pain

Things that hurt our bodies
are so yucky!

What is the worst pain
you've ever had?

Do you have ways to make
yourself feel better?

Good

How can what you wear on the outside make you feel crummy or wonderful on the inside?

When you are wearing something for the first time do people tell you how terrific you look?

Next time you have nothing on at all, look in the mirror and see how wonderful you look then!

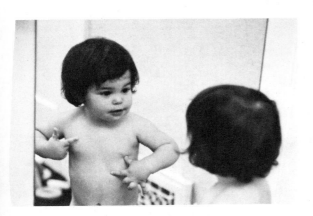

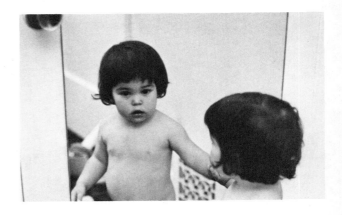

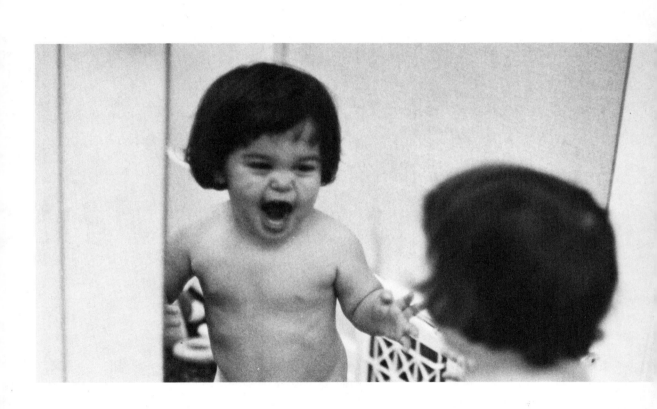

Jealous

Have you ever been so jealous
it made you feel icky inside?

Next time stop and think of the very
special things *only you have!*

In the whole wide world
no one has a thumb print like yours,
or the same inside feelings,
or outloud voice!

And what else is just yours?

Close

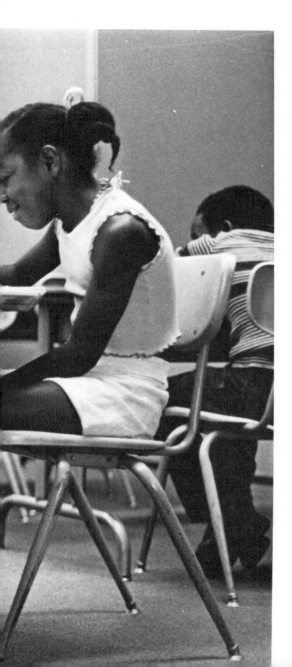

Do inside and outloud things
help you decide you want
to be close friends
with someone?

How do you get to be pals?
When do you KNOW
you really like each other?

Alone

When do you like to be alone?

Have you discovered a place to go where you're really by yourself?

You have explored
ten different feelings
in this book:

1. Special
2. Frustrated
3. Private
4. Fear
5. Love
6. Pain
7. Good
8. Jealous
9. Close
10. Alone

Which of these ten
feelings would you use
to tell a story
about this picture?

Special

How do you *know*
if you're making someone
feel special?

What is the nicest thing
you ever did for someone else?

Frustrated

When you are standing in line do bigger people sometimes get right in front of you?

How do you feel inside?

Practice what you might say outloud.

Private

If you were going to hide a
secret nifty treasure,
what would it be?

Where would you hide it
so no one could even
get a peek?

Fear

Draw a picture of the scariest dream you've ever had.

Are there inside and outside ways your body reacts when you are really frightened?

What helps you calm down?

Love

Is it possible to love someone you are fighting with?

After fights what are some good ways to make up?

Why is it so hard to say, "I was wrong."

How does this picture make you feel inside?

Ask two LITTLE PEOPLE and two BIG PEOPLE how this same picture makes *them* feel inside?

Pain

It can be awfully painful inside
when feelings get hurt.

What is the meanest of mean things
anyone ever said to you?

Pretend you are telling that person OUTLOUD
how those mean words made you feel inside.

Good

Do some days feel good inside from the very beginning?

What do you like to do best of all?

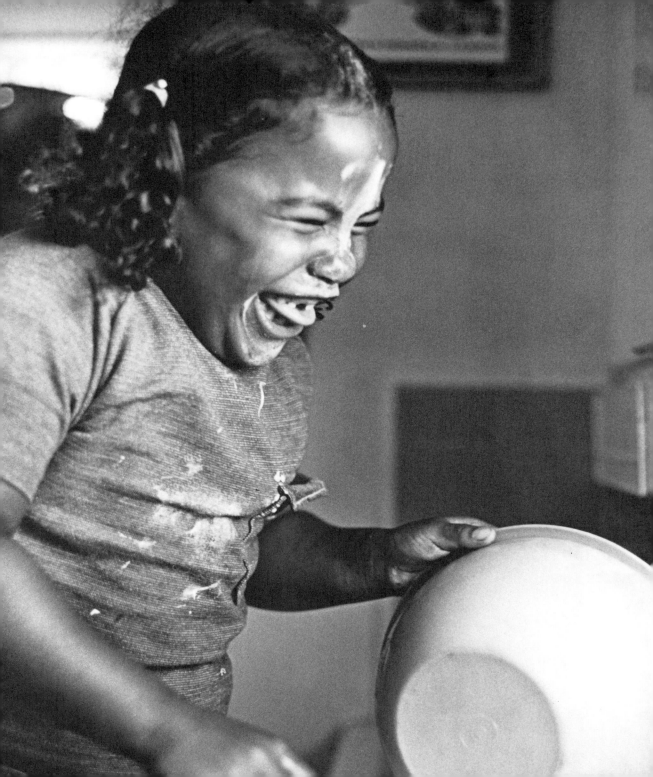

What is something you do so well that others might wish they could do it just like you?

Why are some things so easy and other things so difficult?

Jealous

Close

Friends say, "Wanna play?" and for sure you do . . . . then they go off and leave you out.

Try describing how that makes you feel inside.

When people you like a lot are VERY sad, how do you feel?

Alone

Even when you're with lots of people have you ever felt all alone?

How could you take care of yourself when you are feeling the sad kind of loneliness?

Draw a picture of a sad, lonely person.

Here is one last picture
for your own story.

Can you make up
a different story too?

Here are some tiny
clippings from pictures
in this book.

Use any feelings you want
to tell stories about
these little pictures.

As you went through
this book which feelings
did you like thinking about
the most?

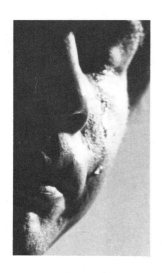

Remember when this book began it said, "It doesn't matter if you are VERY BIG or very little, everyone has inside feelings!" For sure that's true and now you have explored some of your feelings.

One night just before you fall asleep, try figuring out how many different feelings you had that day. Then try to remember which ones you kept tucked inside and which ones your body or your voice told someone else about.

It's time to end this book but just in case you have an inside feeling you want to share, draw a picture or write a letter — the address is on the back of this book.

Craig, who took all of the wonderful pictures for you, joins me in sending you feelings of INSIDE and OUTLOUD LOVE!!

— Barbara Kay Polland

Also by Barbara Kay Polland, Ph.D.

Grandma and Grandpa Are Special People

This book for children and adults alike is about grandparents. Because grandparents have lived a long time, they have a lot of memories to share. This book is about getting to know grandparents—what they are, who they are, what their special role in our lives can be.

Especially geared toward youngsters, this book is instructive, warm, and heart-opening. Filled with tender illustrations.

''For every adult and child who had a grandma and grandpa who tweaked their nose, baked raisin cookies, or toddled them on their knee, and for all those others who wished they had.'' —Virginia Satir

80 pages, 7×8½, $7.95, quality paperback;
ISBN 0-89087-343-7.

To order please send $7.95 plus $1.50 postage and handling to: Celestial Arts, P.O. Box 7327, Berkeley, CA 94707. (CA residents please add 6.5% sales tax.)

Barbara K. Polland, Ph.D., is a credentialed elementary school teacher, a licensed marriage, family, and child therapist, and an associate professor in the Inter-disciplinary Major in Child Development at California State University, Northridge. Dr. Polland brings a rich background as educator, therapist, and mother to all of her books.